Introduction

Picture of an Arapaho camp circa 1870

The Arapaho

From the "Trail of Tears" to Wounded Knee and Little Bighorn, the narrative of American history is incomplete without the inclusion of the Native Americans that lived on the continent before European settlers arrived in the 16th and 17th centuries. Since the first contact between natives and settlers, tribes like the Sioux, Cherokee, and Navajo have both fascinated and perplexed outsiders with their history, language, and culture. In Charles River Editors' Native American Tribes series, readers can get caught up to speed on the history and culture of North America's most famous native tribes in the time it takes to finish a commute, while learning interesting facts long forgotten or never known.

One of the most influential Native American tribes on the Great Plains was the Arapaho, a group so renowned among neighboring Native Americans that it's believed their name came from a Pawnee word for "trader. Like other notable Plains tribes, the Arapaho split off from other groups around the 16th-17th centuries and shifted from a sedentary agricultural society to the kind of nomadic group many envision when thinking of groups on the Plains. That nomadic lifestyle brought them into contact with the Sioux and Cheyenne, both of whom became allies as white settlers pushed west and led to conflicts.

The United States sought to defuse tensions with natives during the westward push by drafting treaties regarding major pieces of land, often without understanding the complex structure of the various tribes, and subgroups within those tribes. Most notably, the Arapaho were victims of the Sand Creek Massacre in 1864, an action considered so heinous that the leader of the attack, Colonel John Chivington, was actually relieved of command after it. Ultimately, the Arapaho were forced onto reservations alongside the Shoshone, one of the tribes Lewis and Clark encountered on their historic expedition in the early 19th century. Today, they are jointly recognized with the Cheyenne, a group they were closely associated with for centuries.

Native American Tribes: The History and Culture of the Arapaho comprehensively covers the culture and history of the famous group, profiling their origins, their history, and their lasting legacy. Along with pictures of important people, places, and events, you will learn about the Arapaho like you never have before, in no time at all.

Native American Tribes: The History and Culture of the Arapaho

By Charles River Editors

Flag of the Arapaho Nation

About Charles River Editors

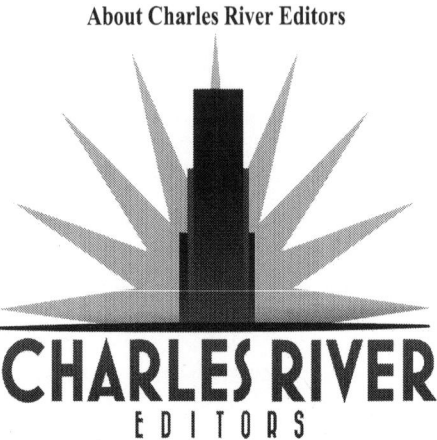

Charles River Editors was founded by Harvard and MIT alumni to provide superior editing and original writing services, with the expertise to create digital content for publishers across a vast range of subject matter. In addition to providing original digital content for third party publishers, Charles River Editors republishes civilization's greatest literary works, bringing them to a new generation via ebooks.

Introductory Note

Spelling of proper names of individuals, various Native American groups, and geographic locations can vary due to historical, cultural, and linguistic tradition. In this text, application of the singular "Arapaho" rather than Arapahos is used according to scholarly, anthropological criteria, notwithstanding the fact that several Arapaho subgroups use the plural.

While the term "tribe" is widely considered socially insensitive and historically inaccurate, it is applied here in deference to the Arapaho Nation, branches of which refer to itself as such.

Chapter 1: The Arapaho Identity

The Arapaho/Arapahoe (*uh-RAP-uh-ho*) people are an Algonquian-speaking indigenous group thought to have migrated from the northeast, probably from the headwaters of the Mississippi River in what is today Saskatchewan, Canada, before making their way to the Great Plains. The Algonquian linguistic family encompasses some 100 different Native American groups, including the Cheyenne and Blackfoot of the Plains, Ojibwe and Shawnee of the Central Region, and Aberaki and Munsee of the East. Although there is no definitive etymological understanding of the name "Arapaho," according to accepted interpretations, it derived from the Pawnee word for "trader" and/or the Crow term for "tattooed people." Regardless, the Arapaho refer to themselves as *Hiinono'ei*, which various sources have translated as meaning "our people," "wrongrooters," or, "cloud people".

In the early 19th century, the Arapaho separated into two largely independent tribal entities, called the Northern and Southern Arapaho, but prior to that, Arapaho territory extended from the Big Horn Mountains of northern Wyoming, south to the Arkansas River, and east to west from the Black Hills to the Rocky Mountains. This giant territory includes parts of modern-day western Nebraska and Kansas, southeastern Wyoming, and eastern Colorado. The separation of the tribe took place centuries after the division of the Arapaho and Gros Ventre (termed in Algonquian oral history as *Arapaho-Gros Ventre* people), two groups believed to have once constituted a single indigenous group that had previously separated from one Algonquian-speaking group.

Today, the Northern Arapaho reside primarily in Wyoming, with their principal communities including Arapahoe, St. Stephens, and Ethete on the Wind River Indian Reservation, while the Southern Arapaho are based in Oklahoma, living primarily in rural areas near the towns of Canton, Greenfield, and Geary in Blaine County, and at Colony in Washita County. Members of the Northern Arapaho refer to the Oklahoma group as Nawathi'neha, meaning "Southerners." Modern anthropologists also group the Gros Ventre people, who today reside on the Fort Belknap Indian Reservation in Montana, with the two Arapaho divisions.

Chapter 2: The Great Plains Culture

Social Structure

Among the various subgroups of the Great Plains Culture, regardless of the adaptive elements of their individual spiritual perspective, most groups traditionally kept large and prominent bundles of sacred objects known as "Medicine Bundles." Varying considerably from group to group, each bundle had its accompanying mythology describing how it was entrusted to an individual of that tribe by supernatural beings or the "Great Spirit" himself, with most claiming theirs to be the one true "Medicine Bundle". This bundle was believed to confer medicinal or magical powers upon the current caretaker. Accordingly, the Blackfeet had their highly ornate "Beaver" and "Pipe Bundles," the Pawnee had their "Star Bundles" (said to contain fossils and fragments of heavenly-sent meteorites), the Cheyenne had their "Sacred Buffalo Hat/Bundle" (which according to some accounts contained four sacred arrows), and the Arapaho had their "Sacred Tribal Flat Pipe/Bundle". The Sacred Tribal Flat Pipe/Bundle was said to have been so powerful that it was housed in its own special teepee and suspended in the air so that it would never touch the ground. Keepers of these bundles were viewed with awe by fellow tribesmen and regarded as more powerful than ordinary shaman; they typically officiated over major ceremonies such as the Sun Dance and the "Buffalo Dance".

In contrast to the sedentary cultures of the Missouri River such as the Mandan, Hidatsa, and Arikara, whose lifestyle afforded a cyclical calendar of ceremonies, rituals and rites, the purely nomadic groups of the Plains tended to only come together twice a year, during spring and summer, for tribal buffalo/bison hunts, to enact the Sun Dance, and to reorganize their military societies. Thus, all known Plains Culture groups included various societies or fraternities (as they are categorized by sociologists) of varying complexity. When cross-tribal camps were organized, a vast array of chiefs, hunters, soldiers, warriors, shaman, conjurers, elders, and band leaders could be present.

Before the Plains tribes adapted them, these "societies" are believed to have first developed among the indigenous Missouri River cultures, including the Otoe, Missouria, Omaha, Ponca, Brulé, Lakota/Sioux, Arikara, Hidatsa, Mandan, Assiniboine, Gros Ventre and Blackfeet. Most societies were age-graded, with children encouraged to join and progress through the ranks as they met age qualification. Children of more affluent families, including girls in some settings, typically purchased the associated society regalia, and the additional rights it afforded them, from older members. The Arapaho were not known to organize their entire society according to age-grade like the Hidatsa and Mandan are believed to have done, but they nonetheless maintained a definite system of "age" societies which at a personal level gave individuals a club where they might socialize with peers, and at the public level it involved them in more important duties. Depending on the setting, these duties could include maintaining organizational cohesion while traveling, overseeing ceremonies, or as it pertained to the highly important buffalo/bison hunts, serving as logistician and quartermaster by distributing supplies and provisions to the hunters.

Among most but not all Plains groups, kinship was bilateral, with the extended family constituting the core of tribal social life. Among the Arapaho, same-sex siblings and opposite-sex siblings-by-marriage were quite open with one another, even to the point of what in some cultures may be considered inappropriate sexual teasing. Opposite-sex adult siblings, however, maintained a highly-respectful distance, even to the point of avoidance; and a similar avoidance was maintained between son-in-law and mother-in-law, as well as father-in-law and daughter-in-law. Communication in these relationships usually required a third party as a go-between. In all known Plains Culture settings, grandparents and elders were held in highest esteem, especially if they held religious or military authority.

According to one myth common to several groups of the Plains, including the Arapaho, men and women surfaced on the Earth via two different lakes and initially lived separately. But since women had no hunting skills (which often left them hungry) and men had no hide-tanning skills (which left them naked and unprotected), Napi ("Old Man"), a Blackfeet hero, decided to bring the two sexes together. Realizing the advantages of the cooperation, men and women decided to make the arrangement permanent; the men agreeing to feed, protect, and provide for the women, and the women agreed to make clothes, tend to the children, and provide for the man within their capacity. Thus, Plains groups see the relationship between men and women as a pact of fair exchange with each requiring the other, making it a natural and necessary symbiotic relationship.

As with most Plains groups, women in Arapaho society were the maintainers of "traditional values", in effect making them the representatives of Arapaho social conscience. In part, this was due to their functional importance in the domestic sphere. Since they maintained the household, cared for the children and prepared the food (which included butchering and dressing the game, and curing the hides for further use), their importance conferred upon them considerable power regarding such issues as rituals and tribal ceremonialism. For example, they were intimately involved in the proceedings of the Sun Dance and even had a voice in discussions regarding "going on the warpath." Arapaho women were known for modesty, attentiveness to duty, and knowledge of "women's work," but Arapaho women could exert strong influence in council even without having an official vote.

That said, there was no ambiguity as to a woman's primary responsibility. For the Arapaho, the words "motherhood" and "woman" were in most dialects the same word or a synonym.

Female Ceremonial Societies

Although women were seldom directly involved with politics and wielded their influence mainly behind-the-scenes, there is no question but that their contribution to the religious realm was important, as was their economic involvement, particularly when it came to horses, the fur trade, and horticulture. Even though the Arapaho were themselves involved in very limited farming, the women regularly traded for cultivated goods. The women also served as arbitrators of trade disputes both among the Arapaho and with other groups

Furthermore, Arapaho women were directly involved with the handling and care of the "Medicine Bundles", as well as other ceremonial rituals and events, such as a chastity and fertility ritual. The women also conducted all family-oriented ceremonies, with the men taking subordinate roles. Thus, as socioanthropologist Katherine Weist observed, "In few other non-Western societies were women able to participate so readily in those male activities that led to high prestige."[1]

For each of the various societal roles women participated in, there was a corresponding ceremonial society, elements of which were known only to society members. During their fertile years, most Arapaho women belonged to one or more societies, and once they were past their childbearing years, they could join male-only societies such as shamanism (though their actual involvement is unclear).

While most Arapaho women belonged to one or more female-only societies, usually connecting ritual and ceremony to food production and fertility/harvests, many also belonged to one or more "buffalo hunting" societies. Women's buffalo societies were highly significant to Arapaho economy and thus integral to neighboring economies. As one trader observed in the 19th century, 'The raw hide of the animal has no trade value. It is only by the woman's skill for putting it in the form of a robe or skin fit for sale that makes its worth." Whether game was plentiful or scarce, the Arapaho and other Plains groups always had to utilize the entire animal. That reality in and of itself made women's skills and knowledge invaluable.

Furthermore, the Plains groups had established a direct sexual/fertility relationship between women and buffalo/bison, chastity and ritual, and fertility and intertribal warfare. Thus, Arapaho men saw themselves as outside the realm of power over life, something controlled by women. Accordingly, women's ceremonial societies served to both enforce the actual and perceived division of abilities and responsibilities between the sexes, as well as empower women as the maintainers of traditional values.

Mating and Marriage

In general, Plains tribes had more interaction with each other than most indigenous cultures of North America, which was at least partly a byproduct of their nomadic nature. But Plains tribes also routinely got together to conduct organized big-game buffalo/bison hunts, perform the Sun Dance, and reorganize their military societies, so it was common for hundreds of marriageable young men and women to find themselves interacting with members of other groups. This

---

[1] *Weist, Katherine M. Plains Indian Woman: An Assessment. Page 262.*

created a challenge for tribes that wanted to maintain both chastity for their women and tribal purity as a whole.

Paradoxically, the Arapaho and other Plains groups encouraged girls of marriageable age to single out young men as potential mates, and young men were also actively encouraged (particularly by their mothers) to seek out, pursue, and essentially target a woman they desired. For example, the Lakota Sioux assigned their daughters *hakatakus*, elder brothers or other male relatives to serve as chaperons and guardians to protect them from the advances of interested males. When it came to choosing a wife, Arapaho boys were told, "[W]hen you want a woman, look for a good young girl. Select one that is good herself and has good parents. [Those who] don't look all around but keep their eyes cast down; girls who always mind their own business."[2] Girls also improved their chances for marriage by learning how to cook and work hides for teepees and clothing, as well as how to make decorative arts (especially beading and quillworking). Among the Arapaho, one of the most important skills a girl learned was the production of fully-beaded moccasins, which required considerable time, skill, and patience. Husbands took great pride in beautifully-crafted moccasins produced by their wives, and women could acquire an additional level of societal status based merely on the extent of their quality.

---

[2] Hilger, Inez. "Arapaho Child Life and its Cultural Background." Page 198.

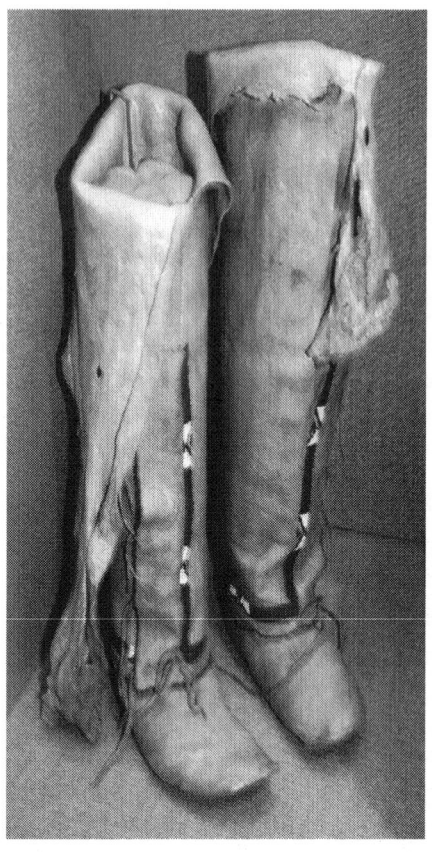

Southern Arapaho moccasins, made in the early 20ᵗʰ century

In most cases, marriages were initiated by the potential husband and a male member of the bride's family, and at least initially, this was often done without the young woman's knowledge. The marriage proposal process typically involved a series of meetings between male members and family elders, during which "bride-price" was discussed. The price typically consisted of a number of horses, tools and/or weapons, and occasionally labor, depending on the wealth and status of the girl's family. The girl herself did not become directly involved until the best possible deal had been struck. Among the Arapaho and Cheyenne, however, should a potential bride flatly refuse to accept the arrangement, the matter generally ended there and then. Foremost among the Arapaho was familial harmony, and unless the intended marriage carried ramifications far beyond the usual, a father would not oppose both daughter and wife. Should the daughter agree, however, negotiations generally continued until the bride-price was sufficiently sweetened. In other words, the bride-price was a bartering process that played out with the father's actual asking price being withheld until the end and the future son-in-law's best offer being withheld until the girl agreed to marry him.

Once the bride-price was delivered, the only wealth a groom brought to a marriage was generated from the acquisition of horses, which were taken during raids and hunts. The value of horses increased considerably when the economic value of a bride was factored in. The bride's family traditionally provided a teepee, most of the furnishings (like back rests and beds), and cooking and eating utensils. After the marriage, the bride retained ownership of these items. To this wealth was added horses gifted or acquired through trade by the wife herself, as well as saddles or other riding tack. Thus, women entered into marriage with considerable possessions and status, and it increased over time as she gained influence over not only her immediate family but the band into which she married.

Birth and Childhood

Virtually every aspect of life had spiritual significance for the Arapaho, so ceremony followed every Arapaho from conception until death. Miscarried fetuses and babies who died during childbirth were considered a whole spiritual being and buried with the same rites and ceremony as an adult. Mothers typically gave birth in the home teepee, from which the family medicine bundles were ritually removed, and she was assisted by her mother or a professional midwife. Mothers generally delivered babies in a kneeling or squatting position while holding on to a horizontal wooden rod positioned over their head. After delivery, the umbilical cord and afterbirth were placed in a special bag, often a beautifully-quilled and beaded bag made by the grandmother or other elder, and that bag was henceforth regarded as a "longevity charm" and typically attached to the baby's cradle for protection. The longevity charm would later become a treasured heirloom kept through generations. An Arapaho woman seldom had more than two children, but a man who could afford more than one wife commonly had one or two children per wife.

Pregnancies were also spaced out because Arapaho children were typically nursed for several years. The Arapaho utilized specially-designed cradles, with the cradles themselves reflecting the cultural and aesthetic ideals of each group, so they varied both in method of construction as well as form. Cradle making was considered a ceremonial act in itself, with their unique quillwork and bead embellishments serving the functional carrying/transporting of the baby, as well as becoming symbols of social prestige within the tribe. While it would be unfair to classify the Arapaho and other Plains groups as materialistic, many material objects acquired spiritual and prestigious attributes once they were crafted and adorned. The Arapaho did not design cradles as elaborate as other Plains tribes like the Sioux, but they did construct some of the most complicated and spiritually-symbolic.

Arapaho cradle

Constructed of several separate pieces of hide sewn together, a large quilled yellow disc (representing the sun) was sewn directly onto the hood, with a band of pendants sewn around the head opening. From the opening hung between 90-100 quilled-wrapped rawhide strips 1mm in width, representing the number of years the maker hoped the child would live. On the yellow disc were sewn red and yellow sections meeting at right angles, symbolizing the Morning Star and/or a woman, four white sections (representing the four corners of the earth), and additional yellow, red, and black elements representing the light of the sun, the heat of the sun, and night respectively. Added to this were four pendants representing the four periods of life (childhood, youth, middle age, and old age) and long strips of buckskin to which bells were sewn, representing a child's energy and movement. The designs certainly varied among the different bands of the Arapaho, but the cradle designs were always complex and full of symbolism.

Children of the Plains tribes were often named for an individual who had lived to an old age or accomplished great deeds, because it was believed namesakes were blessed, but it was unusual for an individual to retain that name throughout life. In some cases, a designated namer was chosen to assign a name to a child, and the naming usually involved an elaborate naming ceremony. During early adulthood, both young men and women personalized their name or had a name foisted upon them (like nicknames) based on characteristics unique to that individual, sometimes in reference to an incident or a commemoration of a special event. It was also not unheard of for Native Americans to acquire a third "white" name, such as Chief "Dan George" Tsleil-Waututh.

One of the first things that caught the attention of early white visitors to Arapaho settlements was the custom of singing to babies. Upon asking the purpose of such songs, typical responses were that lullabies calmed or lulled the children to sleep, entertained the children, or simply because the individual liked to sing. Later ethnographic studies revealed that what were seemingly lullabies were more often songs heard at Plains Indian social events which the child would need to know when they were older, or in the case of sick children, ritual songs related to the Sun Dance believed to carry healing powers. Other songs were simply nonsensical songs similar to those heard in other cultures around the world sang to make children laugh, such as one with the lyric, "beaver teeth, worn out feet, wriggling bags, belly buttons, crabs, and confused fat buffalo calves!"

Arapaho children were indulged and given exceptional freedom, but the Arapaho tactfully directed their children towards activities that instilled cooperation, knowledge of gender-appropriate skills, and spiritual values from the time they could walk. The Arapaho provided play areas where adults only entered when necessary, and children learned life skills through a number of gender-specific games. For example, in the spring, boys were encouraged to play a hoop & stick game in which a wooden hoop laced with rawhide was thrown into the air and players tried to catch it on their sticks. Girls playing a similar game, in which teams of players tried to knock a very ornate ball through the other side's goal. In the summer, both boys and girls were taught to improve their riding and horse-managing skills, and boys fought in make-believe battles wielding toy bows while girls learned childcare using buckskin and bullrush dolls they dressed and carried in small cradles and placed in miniature teepees. The miniature teepees were constructed much like the life-sized ones, complete with smoke flaps. In some settings where dogs were available, puppies took the place of dolls for older girls and were thus dressed and carried in cradles on their backs. In the winter, boys and girls enjoyed sledding, a cooperative endeavor using sleds constructed from rib bones and rawhide. Thus, nearly every activity was both entertaining and culturally relevant, instilling values within the gender roles they would assume throughout life.

Attire

By the 18th century, Arapaho women were renowned for curing hides, developing methods that produced hides far softer and suppler than others. Hides were often painted with green or yellow earth paints and sometimes lightly smoked. Naturally, this meant the Arapaho had some of the most elaborate and stylized attire of all the Native American groups. The Arapaho would utilize virtually every part of the buffalo (hair, hide, bones, sinew) and all the natural world had to offer for fibers, dyes, stones, shells, The clothes would be made from the dressed skins of the buffalo and smaller hoofed animals like the antelope and bighorn sheep.

Before European contact, the standard buffalo robe was the most common garment for both men and women, and it was complemented by a variety of skirts, buckskin dresses, loincloths, moccasins, and side-fold and two-skin women's dresses. These clothes were designed not only with protection in mind but also aesthetic qualities meant to carry social and religious significance. In 1911, after a study of several Plains groups, Harvard ethnologist Alice Fletcher wrote, "The sentiments relating to ancient clothing may be traced, for example . . . to a desire for covering . . . with the motive of differentiating himself [from others], a simple act of self-consciousness expressive of the idea fundamental to costume, decoration, and regalia."[3] Thus, while a spiritual link between an individual's existence and other forms of life was the primary focus, such as men wrapping themselves in buffalo hides to appear like buffalo and have the buffalo transfer their powers to them, there was also an underlying desire for individual recognition by having clothes of such fine quality.

When whites came into contact with the Arapaho, they found that both men and women were styling their hair in two long braids on either side of the head, with the occasional addition of feathers or other ornamentation. At some point in time, Arapaho trade with the neighboring Sioux led some men to choose to wear feathered headdresses.

The Arapaho were also traditionally associated with and recognized by their various war and ceremonial regalia. Although it is today difficult to separate Arapaho ceremonial regalia from other Plains groups, due to items being traded among them, some attire was known to be specific to the Arapaho. This included ceremonial dance kilts (ornate garments associated with age-graded societies), Arapaho lance banners, war bonnets, "Ghost Dance" shirts, and buffalo robes worn by women into battle (the circumstances of which are unclear).

In addition to the fine craftsmanship, the Arapaho often added one of two basic art patterns to their clothes, either abstract geometric designs or lifelike pictographic images. These patterns were applied to everything from functional items such as cradles and teepees to ritual items like medicine bundles and ceremonial shirts, and even practical items like moccasins and robes. Rooted in basic gender roles, males' garments were traditionally decorated with more literal representations, including figures of men, horses, buffalo and other animals, while females' clothes were enlivened with geometrical patterns, the meanings of which were seldom divulged.

One often-referenced Arapaho woman's robe that is currently part of a private collection illustrates what is clearly a direct one-to-one symbolic correspondence with specific elements of a buffalo myth. Complete with physical elements of the mythological buffalo, including its skin, hair, veins, heart, the robe also incorporates detail of the myth itself through representations of the "seven periods of creation," the "pemmican river," the Milky Way galaxy, the "buffalo lodge," and numerous other details. Thus, in some cases, Arapaho designs incorporated aspects of life, myth, and art. Additionally, other garments that initially seem to display simple geometric

---

[3]   Fletcher, Alice Cunningham. Alice Cunningham Fletcher and Francis La Flesche Papers, 1873--1939.

or pictorial representations actually have ancient protection symbols and other types of symbolic iconography.

Food and Food Preparation

Due to the sheer inventiveness and ever-expanding influence shared by women among the Plains groups, they enjoyed a much wider range of foods and food preparation technologies than many other indigenous groups of North America. In addition to normal sources of meat and corn, Plains women learned to make foodstuffs like pemmican, a protein-food with varying ingredients including bison, moose, elk, or deer meat, and fruits such as cranberries, Saskatoon berries, cherries, currants, chokeberries, and blueberries. They also made buffalo jerky by drying meat and making use of a buffalo "paunch," a cooking device in which hot stones were placed into a buffalo-skin sack suspended over a fire via four poles. The paunch could also let women make stews.

Intertribal Interaction

Although most indigenous groups of North America frequently allied in times of famine or conflicts with Europeans and Americans, the Plains tribes had to do so far more often. In addition to forming periodic confederacies to resist common enemies, Plains Indians maintained trade relations with each other, met in frequent council to address common concerns, and joined for hunts and ceremonies at least twice a year. Even warring groups were accustomed to putting differences aside for a number of mutually-beneficial reasons.

Due to the wide variety of languages and dialects commonly spoken among the groups, the Plains tribes developed what was perhaps the most effective system of sign language known to indigenous North America. Regarded as a "universal tongue" among users, which by the 1800s included fur-trading "mountain men", Plains Sign is described as a system of "quick, artful hand movements" that were readily understood by indigenous groups that spanned more than 1,000 miles. Initially, this was handy for negotiating with outsiders, but by the 19th century, the U.S. Army understood the language as well. This made communication easier, but it denied the Plains tribes one of their most valuable negotiating tools. Although the number of signs contained in the system is unknown, oral tradition describes the system as being based on a primary sign, the motion for "Indian," demonstrated by rubbing the fingertips of the right hand twice over the back of the left hand.

Chapter 3: Arapaho Spirituality

Although a complete picture of the Arapaho religion was lost centuries ago, their spiritual worldview can best be understood by comparing it before and after their move to the Plains, and before and after their move to the reservation.

It is widely assumed that before moving south, the Arapaho had much in common with the

Gros Ventre, with whom they shared a sedentary, agrarian lifestyle. That lifestyle generally had an associated mythology that revolved around corn/maize, which was essential to life for them. But after migrating south, they adopted the Plains culture, and the old spiritual worldview was apparently abandoned.

Before moving onto the reservation, the Arapaho people were largely animistic, which meant they believed that spiritual beings inhabit every naturally-occurring thing, including trees, animals, mountains, rivers etc. The spiritual/supernatural realm remained an integral part of their post-Reservation beliefs, but after Christianity was introduced, the Arapaho's worldview was no longer grounded in the traditional beliefs of the Plains Indians.

According to oral tradition, for centuries the Arapaho believed in a powerful and supernatural spirit world that could be accessed via two sacred objects: a ceremonial pipe called the "Flat Pipe" and a wooden hoop referred to as the "wheel". More than just a sacred object, the "Flat Pipe" was recognized as the original being on earth and the means by which the Arapaho could maintain communication with all sacred beings and forces, particularly the "Creator God." Principal entities of the Arapaho universe, each of which had their own realm of power, included the Sun, the Moon, the Earth, Morning Star, Thunderbird, the "Whirlwind Woman," and the "Four Old Men of the Four Directions." Traditional Arapaho also acknowledge various lesser beings and entities that inhabit the Earth, such ghosts and spirits that take various forms.

While shaman and holymen were integral to Arapaho society, there were no formal priests except for during the Sun Dance, so most spiritual power was associated with various societies or fraternities responsible for performing religious ceremonies and enforcing tribal laws. Ultimately, authority for the proper performance of all ceremonies rested in the hands of seven of the oldest men of the tribe, who constituted a sacred society known as "Water-Sprinkling Old Men". This group would hold a daily ceremony in a lodge at the center of camp, but as women became more influential and even became shamans, the power they exerted via their "Buffalo Society" increased as well. The "Water-Sprinkling Old Men" society appears to have diminished in authority as women gained greater control of family ritual.

Although the Arapaho people experienced various spiritual adaptations throughout their history, the greatest changes took place when they moved onto reservations, as new religious traditions emerged to address the severe conditions under which they struggled to survive. These also replaced traditional ceremonies prohibited by federal law. The Sun Dance remained the primary annual ceremony even into modern times, due in part to its perpetuation by other Plains Indians, but in 1890 the Northern Arapaho became the first Plains culture to follow the "Ghost Dance Religion," and by 1900 the Southern Arapaho had adopted the "Peyote Religion". By the mid-20th century, many Arapaho identified with various branches of the Christian religion as well.

For nearly all indigenous Plains tribes, the annual Sun Dance was the most significant religious ceremony of the year, but the Arapaho, Cheyenne, and Sioux practiced the most complex versions of this dance. As such, most modern scholars believe it originated with one or perhaps all of them. The Sun Dance was a quest for supernatural power that was ritualized into a tribal ceremony, and it was believed to ward off famine and enemies. From a sociological perspective, the Sun Dance was not just a religious observance but a secular ceremony designed to reinforce social control.

Traditionally, each summer the various groups of the Plains would gather to reaffirm their basic beliefs and their relationship with the spirit world through words (chants and recitation), ritual acts (like fasting and self-deprivation), and symbolic objects. Pitching their teepees in a great continuous circle, these gatherings sometimes included numerous tribes of the region, with numbers in the thousands, but they could also include just individual groups depending on the political climate at the time, especially after the arrival of the Europeans. In the center of the circle, which represented the sun's supernatural power on earth, a large, open-sided enclosure was built out of upright posts and rafters connected to a towering forked center pole. This area became the focus of the dance.

Men planning to participate in the ritual, usually referred to as initiates or pledgers, would abstain from all food and drink, paint their bodies, and then join a number of dancers in preliminary dances enacted prior to the Sun Dance itself. The movements of the Sun Dance were quite basic, consisting mostly of dancers rising up onto their toes in sync with music played on eagle bone whistles, with pledgers always mindful to face the sun. At the conclusion of the Dance, as an act of self-sacrifice and communion in the name of seeking supernatural power, some participants would commit acts of self-mutilation, while others would dance in a heated frenzy until they collapsed to the ground. In some enactments of the Sun Dance, skewers tethered to the center pole were thrust through the back or chest of the pledger, tearing away people's flesh; the obvious correlation with Christian crucifixion and martyrdom has even led numerous historians to conclude that the Sun Dance was a reaction to exposure to Christian missionaries. Regardless, the Sun Dance continued intermittently for several days and nights, after which the camp was immediately and ceremoniously abandoned. As all of this might suggest, there were plenty of deaths due to dehydration and exhaustion.

By the end of the 19th century, the Sun Dance had spread to 26 known Native American groups, ranging from Saskatchewan, Canada to Texas. In 1904, the federal government outlawed the Sun Dance due to its inherent cruelty and reported casualties, but it was ultimately unable to control it because it was practiced in secrecy. A number of Native American groups carried this ceremony into the 21st century, with several Native revivalist movements reclaiming the practice, albeit in modernized versions.

By the late 1880s, many Native American groups that had been forced to submit to reservation life and were facing severe poverty, starvation, and disease sought a means to revitalize their traditional cultural values. Subsequently, in early 1889 a Paiute shaman named Wovoka, (son of a mystic named Tavibo, claimed he had experienced a religious epiphany during a solar eclipse. Wovoka said he had witnessed the second coming of Jesus Christ and received a warning about the evils of the white man. Word quickly spread that a powerful new "Indian Messiah" had come to liberate them, and numerous tribal representatives were sent to investigate this claim. As professor Gregory Smoak explained, "Shamanism and prophecy were indigenous concepts that created a flexible religious milieu open to the incorporation of new elements and doctrines through the process of direct revelation. The rise of religions based on prophecy explained the radical changes taking place in Native peoples' lives, linked them with other Native peoples, and gave hope that a distinctly 'Indian' way of life would continue."[4]

Some scholars believe the subsequent "Ghost Dance Religion" that sprang up was actually a concerted effort on the part of several Native American leaders to neutralize the rising power of shaman and medicine men. But a short time later, word spread that an Arapaho hunting party had seen the messiah as well, complete with a crown of thorns. Now convinced that this was in fact the reincarnation of Jesus Christ, and that Christ had returned to save them from the whites, delegations from several tribes (including the Arapaho) were sent to visit Wovoka in western Nevada. Upon their return, they brought word of the "Ghost Dance", named for its association with resurrection and reunion with the dead, and these new adherents preached that this new messianic religion would revitalize all the Native American peoples. Among the first converts were members of the Winnebago, Oglala Sioux, and Arapaho, who wholeheartedly embraced the new religion and accepted Jesus Christ as the "Indian Messiah."

According to Wovoka, native peoples had brought hardship upon themselves by their own sins, which opened the cosmic door for white invasion, and salvation could only be achieved by purging themselves of the evil learned from the white man (especially alcohol) by engaging in frequent ceremonial cleansing, chanting, meditation, prayer, and the Ghost Dance itself. Through the Ghost Dance, the Earth would be destroyed and the whites would be wiped off the land and buried beneath the "new soil of the spring that would cover the land and restore the prairie." When this new spring arrived, the buffalo and antelope would return and ancestors would rejoin them from the afterlife. Once the natural balance was restored, the land would again be home to the natives, free of the borders and confines imposed by the white man.

The Ghost Dance was usually organized for mid-afternoon or late afternoon, and attendance was mandatory. Those who did not attend were warned of being "turned to stone" or were summarily punished. Directed by a Ghost Dance leader who carried a 6 foot staff decorated with red cloth and red feathers and a selection of priests ordained by conferment of a crow or eagle

[4] Pettigrew, Dawn Karima. "Ghost Dances and Identity: Prophetic Religion and American Indian Ethnogenesis in the Nineteenth Century."

feather, participants were instructed to bathe to rid the body and spirit of all evil and were then ceremoniously painted with intricate signs. These signs were supposedly revealed to the priests in trances, and the paints were in colors of red, yellow, green, and blue, meant to strengthen their spiritual vision and physical health. Following highly choreographed dance steps accompanied by chants and songs, the dancers would move non-stop until they collapsed to the ground in a trance. Upon regaining consciousness, they would relate their visions to the priests for interpretation. The Sioux routinely donned white "Ghost Shirts" when performing this ritual, as did many Arapaho. No metal objects or musical instruments were involved.

Anthropologists who witnessed the Ghost Dance noted the absence of the overt sexual displays typical of Arapaho ceremonies. Although sexuality was closely associated with spirituality in the Arapaho mindset, during the Ghost Dance, sexual behavior was suppressed, with the performers' attention focused entirely on the esoteric purpose of the dance and the "message of salvation" it was said to convey.

By mid-November of 1890, the Ghost Dance had become so prevalent on Sioux reservations that virtually all normal day-to-day activities had stopped. Convinced that the increasing numbers of Ghost Dancers, at one point numbering more than 3,000 from at least a dozen Plains tribes (including the Arapaho), was a precursor to a violent uprising, on December 15, 1890, 43 Indian Police attacked and killed famed Sioux leader Sitting Bull, claiming that he was at the center of the movement. The federal government's documents indicated that the official end of the Ghost Dance Movement came as early as 1891, but like the Sun Dance, the Ghost Dance was practiced in secrecy well into the 20th century.

The use of peyote as a religious sacrament spread to the Plains from the Apache, Navajo, and various tribes in the Southwest. Its popularity is often attributed to Quanah Parker, who started the "Peyote Religion Movement" in the 1880s, and it eventually led to the founding of the Native American Church in Oklahoma in 1918. Parker claimed to have adopted the peyote religion after being gored by a bull in South Texas and surviving the attack with the help of peyote tea provided by a Coahuiltecan, a Mexican healer or shaman. That healer then healed him and guided him in a formal peyote ceremony.

Subsequently, Parker taught followers that sacred peyote medicine, acquired via the peyote "button", was a sacrament given all peoples by the "Creator God" and was to be used when taking communion in Native American Church medicine ceremonies. It is unclear how or when the Peyote Religion was introduced to the Southern Arapaho, but it was being practiced by 1900, so it was likely well-known to all indigenous populations on Oklahoman reservations by then. While specific beliefs varied from tribe to tribe today, most Arapaho peyotists believed peyote personified a god called *Mescalito,* who in some circles was interpreted as Jesus Christ, perhaps due to the earlier association with the Ghost Dance Religion. Other orders believe there is a peyote deity who acts as a spiritual guardian. Either way, the "Peyote Road" calls for Native

Americans to embrace brotherly love, often in the form of Native American nationalism, family care, self-support through employment, avoidance of alcohol, and avoidance of recreational use of peyote.

Death and the Afterlife

Before moving onto reservations, the deceased were buried within the same day as death, with only the immediate family witnessing the ceremony. The dead were traditionally buried in a stone-covered grave wearing his or her best traditional attire and a number of personal belongings, while remaining personal possessions were either burned or bequeathed to close relatives. The deceased's teepee or dwelling was typically abandoned or ceremoniously burned, and if the deceased was a warrior, his best horse was killed and left at the gravesite.

According to the Arapaho, the deceased's spirit lingered among its family and friends for four days before traveling to hiyei'in, a destination often translated as "our home" and located "above and somewhere to the west". For one year following a death, close male relatives maintained mourning behavior by appearing in public unkempt, and wives and mothers often withdrew from public life altogether. In some settings, Arapaho women gashed their legs or stomachs or sacrificed a portion of a finger.

Chapter 4: 19th Century Conflict

The Arapaho were known as "Cloud Men" by the Cheyenne, "Blue Cloud Men" by the Sioux, and Ahyato by the Kiowa, and as the western-most member of the Algonquian-speaking collective, the Arapaho became a dominant trading group soon after arriving in the Great Plains around the 17th or 18th century. Oral tradition speaks little of pre-Plains history, and archaeological evidence is scant, but it is assumed that prior to coming to the Plains, the Arapaho had established villages near the headwaters of the Mississippi River and cultivated corn/maize to support a sedentary lifestyle. The lifestyle changes that came with moving south may account for the loss of ancient oral history.

Once they reached the Plains, they adopted the highly-mobile, nomadic buffalo-hunter habits common to the other groups living there. After the acquisition of the horse, which likely took place even before they actually came into contact with the Europeans, the Arapaho lifestyle changed yet again. Able to travel farther and hunt buffalo more efficiently, they were able to dominate the trade system in place when Europeans arrived.

One of the earliest written accounts of the Arapaho people described them as "a group divided into seven age-graded ritual societies" whose religion was based on a "bundle containing a tubular pipe as a tribal fetish." In 1780, the Arapaho population was estimated at 3,000, which is ironically the same number who would identify themselves as Arapaho in the 1970 census. Splitting soon after first contact with the Europeans, the Northern Arapaho settled in Eastern

Wyoming while the Southern Arapaho settled in Colorado, and each group formed alliances with other tribes. The Arapaho had a pattern of shifting, separating, and adapting, but this major division was primarily the result of the so-called "friendly treaty" that the Lakota Sioux and Cheyenne had signed allowing wagon trains to pass through their territory unmolested. Due to that agreement, within just a few years, a barren strip had been blazed through the middle of common hunting grounds, effectively dividing the once massive buffalo/bison herd into two; one migrating north, and the other moving south.

In 1834, two ambitious fur traders named William Sublette and Robert Campbell established the Fort Laramie trading post at the junction of the Laramie and North Platte rivers in modern-day southeastern Wyoming. This trading post went up in the heart of the Arapaho hunting grounds, and it instantly became the most popular trading post on the Central Plains. In 1836, it was purchased by the American Fur Company, which recognized the region as a "beaver trappers' paradise", and the post soon drew the attention of the Northern Arapaho, who subsequently set up camp near the post to participate in the flourishing fur trade.

By the summer of 1843, however, the southeastern Wyoming landscape and the thriving Fort Laramie trade system changed dramatically as the first sizable Oregon migration brought thousands of settlers passing through. Within just three years, the fur trade took a drastic downturn as priorities shifted from commerce to protection of the influx of settlers, which now included considerable numbers of Mormons and gold seekers en route to California. These settlers routinely stopped at the Fort for refreshments and occasionally needed protection from hostile natives.

Citing the need to provide permanent protection for the settlers passing through "Indian Country," in 1849 the U. S. Government bought the Fort and transformed it into a military post, garrisoning 200 soldiers. Almost immediately, the formerly friendly trading post became a sprawling military installation designed to resist Indian attack, with the Arapaho, Cheyenne, and Lakota Sioux who had become accustomed to interacting with whites now suddenly unwelcome. This was just the first in a long succession of trading forts purchased by the federal government and converted into military installations.

By 1851, fear and panic spread throughout the Plains populations. Not only were Americans no longer interested in trade relations, as evidenced by the exponential buildup of military bases, but they had effectively disrupted intertribal trade routes, killed or scared off much of the game, and introduced diseases like smallpox, measles, cholera, and whooping cough for which the indigenous populations had no immunity. That summer, General William S. Harney convened a meeting, calling various tribes to Fort Laramie to negotiate territorial and "right-of-way" issues through their territory. More than a dozen Plains tribes, several of which were generational sworn enemies, called a temporary intertribal truce to meet with representatives at Fort Laramie and address the disruption whites had brought to the Plains. To the Native Americans, a treaty was a negotiating process: the stating of one's position, hearing the opponent's arguments, proffers of compromise, and then deciding to accept or reject the treaty. The chiefs had assumed that at a minimum they would have the opportunity to make their concerns known. About 30 miles east of the Fort in the meadows at the mouth of Horse Creek, an estimated 10,000 Arapaho, Sioux, Cheyenne, Crow, Assiniboine, Mandan, Brule (Lakota), Hidatsa, Arikara, Shoshone, and smaller bands came to negotiate, which was possibly the largest gathering of Native Americans on the Plains in history.

U.S. officials wanted the Native Americans to end intertribal warfare to achieve Harney's goal of allowing settlers to pass through the region in safety. As a result, the general was ordered to obtain permission from the Native American leaders for settlers traveling through native lands en route to the Pacific Coast. This became even more imperative when the California Gold Rush of 1849 led that many more people west in search of riches.

General Harney

The government solution was to assign each band a defined territory where they were to remain, but such types of negotiation were meaningless to the Plains tribes, who mostly failed to see the validity made without the consensus of all involved. With 300 U. S. Army mounted infantry and rifles at the ready, 27 wagonloads of various gifts were brought to the chiefs, but their actual concerns were largely ignored. Nonetheless, by September 17, 1851, the tribal council decided it was in their best interest to sign a non-aggression pact with the federal government, as well as between themselves. In exchange for annual payments of $50,000 and recognition of "traditional territorial claims" as agreed upon by the tribes themselves, the

Arapaho, Cheyenne, Sioux, Crow, Assiniboine, Mandan, Hidatsa, and Arikara nations guaranteed safe passage for settlers on the Oregon Trail. Nevertheless, the Sioux is the only group known to have actually received compensation, and while the Native Americans consented to the creation of roads and even forts along the route, they did not consent to settlers encroaching on the lands marked for them, which would inevitably happen as the federal government turned a blind eye.

By the mid-1850s, the Fort Laramie Treaty of 1851 had been rendered largely meaningless. A number of Native American bands who were unaware of the existence of the treaty continued their traditional and annual raiding against other Native American bands, and white settlers continually trespassed through native territory in violation of the treaty's stipulations. While many soldiers were sent to protect the settlers, the government also instituted a policy to starve out the Plains groups by encouraging buffalo soldiers like the famous "Buffalo" Bill Cody to decimate buffalo herds. As the buffalo were being exterminated, other American agents were sent to bribe the more congenial groups into relocating to government-established reservations with promises of food, clothing, and medicine. Those who complied soon discovered that they were given shabby clothes and not enough rations.

In 1854, various Sioux bands were encamped near Fort Laramie when an emaciated cow wandered into the mixed Lakota Sioux camp. In such mixed gatherings, Native Americans assumed a very forgiving and conciliatory attitude toward one another, a politeness that sought to avoid unnecessary conflict. A Miniconjou warrior named High Forehead soon slaughtered and processed the animal, but it turned out the bovine had escaped from a Mormon wagon train migrating west. Shortly after, the animal's owner approached Lieutenant John Fleming, the senior officer at Fort Laramie, reporting that Native Americans had stolen his cow.

Fleming summoned Conquering Bear to the fort to discuss the matter, because Conquering Bear was the Brule Lakota warrior who had been arbitrarily named a "chief" by the American representatives during the Fort Laramie treaty council in 1851. They had demanded a single representative from each group with which to deal, and when the indigenous people did not acknowledge a single leader, they appointed leaders for them. When Conquering Bear arrived at Fort Laramie, he tried to negotiate compensation for the cow, offering several ponies from his personal herd or a cow from the band's herd, understanding that the conditions of the Fort Laramie Treaty rendered this matter to the Indian Agent. The Mormon migrant refused these offers and instead demanded $25, and Lieutenant Fleming gave in to the Mormon demand that the offending Native American, High Forehead, be arrested. To do so he dispatched his subordinate to the Lakota camp to arrest the offending warrior. Second Lieutenant John L. Grattan was ready and willing to lead a force to arrest High Forehead, but both he and his commander were unaware that these types of matters had been delegated to the local Indian Agent and were not the purview of the military.

A photo of Fort Laramie in the 1850s

The appointed agent had not yet arrived in the area, so on August 29, 1854, Grattan led a force of twenty-nine soldiers, interpreter Lucien Auguste, and two cannons to the Lakota encampment. Auguste was greatly disliked by the Lakota and drank heavily on the way to the camp, arriving very drunk. As the soldiers entered the camp, Auguste began taunting the warriors, calling them women and saying that the soldiers had come to kill, not to negotiate. Grattan broke Auguste's bottle and openly berated him, indicating that he likely understood the danger of the situation his force faced. The encampment was populated by an estimated 4,800 mixed Lakota people and about 1,200 warriors.

James Bordeaux, who owned the nearby trading post, was consulted and advised Lieutenant Grattan to speak directly with Conquering Bear and allow the Native American leadership to handle the situation. Although Bordeaux reported that Grattan seemed to understand, the young, recent West Point graduate went directly to High Forehead's lodge and demanded his surrender. When High Forehead refused, Grattan then went to Conquering Bear and demanded that he hand over High Forehead. The warrior refused because he had no authority over the Miniconjou and did not want to violate the tradition of hospitality extended to visitors from other bands.

The negotiations went on for some time, with the drunken Auguste speaking broken Dakota since he had no knowledge of other dialects. As Grattan pushed Conquering Bear to hand over High Forehead, warriors moved into flanking positions around the soldiers. Exasperated, Grattan ended the discussion and began walking back to his column. As he walked, one of the nervous troops fired a shot that struck a Lakota warrior. Chaos ensued and a firefight broke out, during which Conquering Bear was shot in the back and died nine days later. Grattan, Auguste, and the rest of the soldiers were soon dead. As the fight progressed a group of about eighteen soldiers tried to break out and reach the safety of some nearby rocks, but they were run down and killed by a group of warriors led by Red Cloud. The enraged Native Americans then looted the trading post but did not hurt Bordeaux, whom they regarded as a friend.

In the aftermath of what newspapers would call the Grattan Massacre, the massive Native American camp disbanded and left for their respective hunting grounds. The Grattan Massacre became a catalyst for a generalized hostility between whites and Plains Indians that would last for over two decades, but despite the obvious implications of the Grattan Massacre, at first there was no real reaction or retribution from the U.S. Army and government. Intertribal warfare between Sioux bands and their Cheyenne and Arapaho enemies resumed around 1860, but it was not until after 1862, when Union Pacific Railroad workers began surveying a route through the southern buffalo hunting grounds, that trouble arose. The Native Americans relied on summer buffalo hunts and feared that the railroad running directly through their southern hunting grounds would disrupt the annual hunt. Numerous Plains people of many different tribes met at these southern hunting camps during the annual summer hunt, and despite current animosities they met together to celebrate feasts and to hold joint councils.

Pressed now on three sides by whites and native enemies, the Comanche took a bold and decisive step by forming an alliance with the Arapaho and Cheyenne and several lesser indigenous bands that would become known as "The Great Peace". This was a pact that stopped all intertribal warfare between them so that all Plains warriors were free to direct their attention to stopping both white and native intruders. As a result, by the late 1850s, "the Alliance" was able to regain control of much of the Plains, successfully and defiantly resisting American military forces sent to disrupt them.

Nevertheless, with buffalo/bison herds quickly diminishing in size, competition for food resulted in raids by Native Americans against each other in Kansas and Texas. Meanwhile, the Civil War prevented American soldiers mostly from fighting Native Americans, so the Arapaho/Comanche/Cheyenne alliance was essentially free to execute justice as they saw fit.

In 1861, Colorado governor John Evans convinced two Southern Cheyenne "peace" chiefs, Black Kettle (*Moketarato*) and White Antelope (*Vó'kaa'e Ohvó' komaestse*) to sign an agreement that surrendered a large tract of hunting land near what was becoming the thriving settlement of Denver in present-day Colorado. White Antelope was a highly-vocal follower of the teachings of

Sweet Medicine, who said that chiefs are to be peacemakers; and he saw it as his spiritual duty not to advocate violence or incite controversy in any form. However, most other Cheyenne chiefs rejected further intrusion by whites and refused to sign any new agreement.

Hoping to goad the Cheyenne into a confrontation, in the spring of 1864, the Colorado Militia launched a series of unprovoked attacks on Cheyenne camps. The militia was led by Colonel John Chivington, a "fire and brimstone" Methodist minister and renowned Indian-hater who had publicly advocated indiscriminately killing "Indian" children because "nits makes lice". Warning his men ahead of battle, Chivington stated, "Damn any man who sympathizes with Indians! I have come to kill Indians and believe it is right and honorable to use any means under God's heaven to kill Indians!"

Chivington

As historian Dee Brown noted in the seminal *Bury My Heart at Wounded Knee*, at this time, "(Northern Cheyenne leader) Roman Nose and a number of Dog Soldier Cheyenne went north for better hunting in Powder River country with their Northern Cheyenne cousins . . . (while) Black Kettle, White Antelope, and Lean Bear kept their bands below the Platte." But when Major Edward Wynkoop, commander of Fort Lyon (Colorado), heard that Chivington had ordered his men to 'kill Cheyenne whenever and wherever found,' he sent word to Black Kettle and White Antelope and invited them to move their bands closer to the fort, partly to protect them from being targeted and partly to prevent them from being provoked into all-out war.

However, this plan backfired when Chivington replaced the "too conciliatory" Wynkoop with Major Scott Anthony, who encouraged the Cheyenne to make camp nearby. Unlike Wynkoop's plan to move the Cheyenne closer to the fort to protect them and prevent war, Anthony's plan was to make it easier to target the Cheyenne for a slaughter.

A picture of Black Kettle and some of his followers on September 28, 1864. The picture captures what Black Kettle thought was a peace council with Governor Evans and Chivington. Wynkoop is kneeling on the left. White Antelope is first on the left in the middle row, and Black Kettle is third from left in the middle row.

On the morning of November 29, 1864, Colonel Chivington led 700 men in a surprise attack against Black Kettle's camp at Sand Creek. According to Cheyenne oral tradition and several surviving soldiers' accounts, as soon as Black Kettle saw the army coming, he raised an American flag on a pole and waved it back and forth calling out that his *Wutapai* band was not resisting. Ignoring his cries for mercy, the soldiers commenced firing, -cutting down an estimated 70-200 Cheyenne, about two-thirds of whom were women and children. The Cheyenne claimed that soldiers shot babies in the head at point-blank range, raped Cheyenne women, and scalped dead warriors. The following morning, Army Lieutenant James Connor, who had refused to follow Chivington's orders, visited the scene of the massacre, and he reported:

"In going over the battleground the next day I did not see a body of man, woman, or child but was scalped, and in many instances their bodies were mutilated in the most horrible manner - men, women, and children's privates cut out . . . I heard one man say he cut out a woman's private parts and had them for exhibition on a stick . . . I also heard of numerous instances in which men had cut out the private parts of females and stretched them over saddle-bows and wore them over their hats while riding in the ranks."[5]

Black Kettle had managed to escape the slaughter, only to be killed during George Custer's unprovoked attack at Washita River in 1868, but White Antelope was killed and his body was mutilated. According to historian Stan Hoig in *The Sand Creek Massacre*, "The body of White Antelope, lying solitarily in the creek bed, was a prime target. Besides scalping him the soldiers cut off his nose, ears, and testicles - the last for a tobacco pouch."[6]

The results of the massacre were precisely what Colonel Chivington hoped to achieve. The Cheyenne, who were at this time allied with the Lakota and Arapaho, vowed to avenge the needless deaths of Black Kettle and his people. Early in 1865, a coalition of 1000 Cheyenne, Lakota Sioux, and Arapaho attacked several white ranches and a military post along the South Platte River Trail near Denver, capturing wagon-trains, confiscating livestock, and killing several hundred white settlers in the process. Staying one step ahead of the U. S. Army, they continued to raid the North Platte Trail that summer, completely wiping out an Army wagon-train and taking its horses and supplies. In response, the U. S. Government dispatched General P. E. Connor and a force of 3,000 men with orders to ignore any overtures of peace or compliance from the marauders, and to "kill every male Indian over the age of 12".

Since this order was coming on the heels of the Civil War, the U.S. Army was still in some disarray, and the Cheyenne/Lakota Sioux/Arapaho Alliance managed to stay beyond their reach for the next two years. Meanwhile, under the "Little Arkansas Treaty," the Southern Cheyenne and Southern Arapaho tribes were granted portions of Kansas and a section of "Indian Territory" in present-day Oklahoma as a reservation.

Near the end of 1867, the U. S. government brought the Cheyenne and Arapaho to a council once again in the hopes of establishing peace through the "Medicine Lodge Treaty", which was actually three treaties signed in October 1867. The terms provided the Arapaho with their own reservation in Kansas, but they initially rejected that and subsequently agreed instead on a site in "Indian Territory" (present-day Oklahoma) near Fort Reno, to be jointly-shared with the Southern Cheyenne.

However, some of the Southern Cheyenne resisted, and when American efforts did not produce

---

[5] *Wilson, James.* The Earth Shall Weep. *Page 274.*
[6] *Hoig, Stan.* The Sand Creek Massacre. *Page 153.*

the desired end, plans were made to use military force against the Plains tribes. In 1867, Major General Winfield Scott Hancock, a Union hero at Gettysburg, decided that the best tactic to force the Native Americans into compliance was to single out and make an example of one group, which would theoretically intimidate the others to fall in line or face the consequences. Hancock marched 1,400 battle-hard soldiers into a Cheyenne/Sioux encampment without warning, and hysteria and panic ensued as the memory of Sand Creek sent hundreds of men, women, and children fleeing into the countryside while Hancock burned the village to the ground.

In July of 1867, U. S. Congress implemented a "General Peace Policy" aimed at "abolishing Indian wars forever by removing their causes." Traveling first to North Platte, Nebraska to confer with the Oglala (Sioux), Brule (Sioux) and Northern Cheyenne, U. S. representatives attempted to convince tribal leaders to abandon their nomadic lifestyle and take up farming. This, they reasoned, would remove the contention that was leading to interfering in the construction of the railroads and attacks made on frontier settlements. They then met with bands of the Arapaho, Comanche, Kiowa, Cheyenne, and Plains Apache, convincing them to convene at Medicine Lodge Creek in southern Kansas to formalize an agreement. Meeting as agreed, the parties signed the "Medicine Lodge Treaty" of 1867, with the Cheyenne and Arapaho granted lands constituting the Cheyenne and Arapaho Indian Reservation, an expanse of land less than half the size provided by the "Little Arkansas Treaty".

Despite what the "Medicine Lodge Treaty" was intended to resolve, unrest continued as the building of the Kansas and Pacific Railroad further scattered the remaining game and white hunters tracked and killed the remaining buffalo merely for the hides, often leaving the carcass to the vultures and coyotes. Tensions were high, and in late November 1867, George Custer's cavalry tracked down Black Kettle's band of Cheyenne, which culminated in the Battle of Washita near what fittingly became Cheyenne, Wyoming. During the early morning hours of November 27, Custer marched his men and split them in separate groups to converge upon the Cheyenne village, surprising the inhabitants with a charge. Custer's 7th Cavalry suffered about 30 casualties, but in the melee they managed to force many Cheyenne to surrender and shot many more. Custer reported to his superiors that at least 103 Cheyenne warriors were killed in battle, and there were certainly more Cheyenne, including women and children, killed. The American cavalry casualties came while a detachment led by Major Joel Elliot chased fleeing Cheyenne and were overwhelmed by neighboring warriors from nearby camps. When Custer learned that Black Kettle's village was only one of many, he ended his offensive and was content to take the supplies and prisoners from the camp, but many men in the 7th Cavalry were upset that he had not tried to reinforce Elliot, who was killed along with many of his men.

Custer

Once Custer was aware that he was in the vicinity of other Native American warriors, with overwhelming numbers no less, he very conspicuously made it known that he was holding over 50 women and children captive. While they were not technically hostages, Custer was hoping that the nearby Cheyenne wouldn't attack the 7th Cavalry and risk the deaths of their own people. As military historian Larry Skenlar put it, "Custer probably could not have pulled off this tactical coup had he not had in his possession the fifty-some women and children captives. Although not hostages in the narrowest meaning of the word, doubtlessly it occurred to Custer that the family-oriented warriors would not attack the Seventh with the women and children…" Custer admitted as much, writing in his own book, *My Life on the Plains*, "Indians contemplating a battle, either offensive or defensive, are always anxious to have their women and children removed from all danger…For this reason I decided to locate our camp as close as convenient to the village, knowing that the close proximity of their women and children, and their necessary exposure in case of conflict, would operate as a powerful argument in favor of peace, when the question of peace or war came to be discussed."

In light of the fact that many Southern Cheyenne were abiding by the terms and moving onto reservations, the Battle of Washita is often considered an unnecessary battle, and it has even been called a massacre. A publication called the *Leavenworth Evening Bulletin* reported, "Gen. S. Sandford and Tappan, and Col. Taylor of the Indian Peace Commission, unite in the opinion that the late battle with the Indians was simply an attack upon peaceful bands, which were on the march to their new reservations". The *New York Tribune* also noted in early December, "Col.

Wynkoop, agent for the Cheyenne and Arapahos Indians, has published his letter of resignation. He regards Gen. Custer's late fight as simply a massacre, and says that Black Kettle and his band, friendly Indians, were, when attacked, on their way to their reservation."

Although Custer's attack was effective in breaking the spirit of the Cheyenne and Arapaho, and it essentially spelled the beginning of the end of independent life for most Plains Indians, numerous bands continued to wreak havoc whenever they could. In response, a national outcry arose, demanding that remaining members of the Plains Indians be captured and taken to Florida for confinement at Fort Marion in St. Augustine, where they would have no chance of rejoining their people. For the remainder of that year, the United States Army endeavored to round up and remove the remaining Arapaho, Comanche, Kiowa, and Southern Cheyenne to reservations in "Indian Territory", a military campaign that would become known as the "Red River War." More a series of small, armed skirmishes with few casualties than an actual "war," by year's end most free Arapaho had been captured and relocated, with the last renegade group surrendering in mid-1875. The conclusion of the Red River War historically marked the end of the free-roaming Native American populations of the southern Plains.

Chapter 5: Reservation Life

In 1868, the Eastern Shoshone ceded their ancestral lands to the federal government in exchange for land on the Wind River Range of Wyoming, and that was ultimately where the Northern Arapaho moved to. The reservation consists of about 3,475 square miles in west-central Wyoming. The Shoshone live primarily in the west and northwest section, while the Arapaho are settled mainly in the east and southeast. As of 2011, there were 3,737 registered Shoshone and 8177 Arapaho there.

Following the Red River War, nearly all Southern Arapaho and Southern Cheyenne attempted to adapt to reservation life. At the beginning of the reservation period, there were an estimated 1,600 Southern Arapaho living in Oklahoma and about 900 Northern Arapaho living in Wyoming. But despite their best intentions, rations provided by the U. S. Government proved inadequate, and with malnutrition and disease nearly wiped out several bands. Congress underestimated the necessary funds, resulting in poor quality and often sickly cattle. With tensions quickly mounting between the indigenous population and neighboring white ranchers, the U.S. Army thought it best to withhold ammunition, consequently making the Arapaho and Cheyenne horses easy prey for White horse thieves. From 1875-1878, the Arapaho and Cheyenne tried to compete with white buffalo hunters for the last few remaining buffalo, but they had little success.

In the late 1870s to early 1880s, the Arapaho and Cheyenne made concerted efforts to adapt to farming, with the Arapaho proving the more successful of the two. It took several years, however, to fully understand the fundamentals of dry land farming and the necessary methods to conserve winter moisture. Recurrent droughts ultimately resulted in bad crop failures, starvation, and disease. For a short time, there were plans to build a cattle herd, but the plan was soon aborted.

The Southern Arapaho moved onto reservation in Oklahoma alongside the Cheyenne, but the Dawes Act of 1887, which authorized the division of native lands into allotments for individual tribe members, effectively broke up the joint Arapaho-Cheyenne unified land base. Then, in the "Land Run of 1892," all land not allotted to individual Native Americans was opened to white settlement. At noon on April 19, 1892, the lands of the Cheyenne-Arapaho Reservation were opened for settlement, and the Cheyenne and Arapaho only retained about 530,000 acres of the original 3 million acre allotment. This was followed in 1898 by the "Curtis Act," which dismantled tribal governments in an effort to compel the indigenous population to assimilate.

In 1936, the "Oklahoma Indian Welfare Act" was passed, after which the Southern Arapaho and Cheyenne formally organized a single tribal government. In the wake of the "Indian Self-Determination Act of 1975", which was intended to restore Native American autonomy and reverse policies forced upon indigenous groups through U.S. treaties and establishment of the reservation system, the Arapaho-Cheyenne alliance has proven to be one of the most successful and mutually-beneficial relationships among all Native American groups.

Today, the Arapaho Nation is comprised of an estimated 10,000-12,000 members, depending upon the source and depending on whether the Gros Ventre are included. Though anthropologists consider the Gros Ventre part of the Nation, that is a position not held by many modern Arapaho, who acknowledge their ancient ties to that group but consider them separate. Complicating things, the name Gros Ventre has been adopted by two separate Native American groups, the *Gros Ventre/Atsina* (a branch of the Arapaho who share a common language and customs but are more closely related to the Assiniboine people), and the *Gros Ventre/Hidatsa* (a branch of the Crow Nation who live in North Dakota but were closely associated with the Blackfeet during the 19th century, and are today closely associated with the Mandan People).

Even before their independent inception, the Arapaho culture became synonymous with adaptation. Accustomed to migration, transformation, and assimilation, the Arapaho proved themselves resistant to forced change, but ultimately pliable to taking on aspects of other cultures. Though they are a people who could have easily been lost to change or conflict, the Arapaho's will to survive is unquestionably their greatest attribute and most enduring heritage.

Bibliography

Beard, Charles A., and Mary R. Beard. The Beards' New Basic History of the United States. New York: Doubleday & Company, Inc., 1960.

Berthrong, Donald J. The Cheyenne and Arapaho Ordeal: Reservation and Agency Life in the Indian Territory, 1875-1907. OK: University of Oklahoma Press, 1976.

Brown, Dee. Bury My Heart at Wounded Knee. *New York: Holt, Rinehart & Winston, 1970.*

Cheyenne-Arapaho Lands website: http://rebelcherokee.labdiva.com/itcheyenne_arapaho.html. Access 06.27.2013.

Fletcher, Alice Cunningham. Alice Cunningham Fletcher and Francis La Flesche Papers, 1873-- 1939. *Accessed via: http://siris-archives.si.edu/ipac20/ipac.jsp?uri=full=3100001~!82241!0 06.28.2013.*

Hilger, Inez. "Arapaho Child Life and its Cultural Background." Bureau of Ethnology, Bulletin 148. *Washington, D. C.: Smithsonian Institution,1952.*

Indian Affairs: Laws and Treaties (compiled and edited by Charles J. Kappler. Washington: Government Printing Office, 1904). Accessed via: http://digital.library.okstate.edu/kappler/Vol1/HTML_files/IND0839.html 06.27.2013.

Kroeber, Alfred L. The Arapaho. *Nebraska: University of Nebraska Press, 1983. Accessed via http://books.google.com/books?id=KX5_bcr985sC&printsec=frontcover#v=onepage&q&f=fals e 06.26.2013.*
                    Traditions of the Arapaho. *Indiana: Indiana University Library, 1903.*
Accessed via http://books.google.com/books?id=YrPWAAAAMAAJ&printsec=frontcover#v=onepage&q&f=f alse 06.27.2013.

Montana's Official State Website: Fort Belknap Assiniboine (Nakoda) & Gros Ventre (A-a-ni- nin) Tribes: http://tribalnations.mt.gov/fortbelknap.asp Accessed: 06.30.2013.

Neusius, Sarah, W., and G. Timothy Gross. Seeking Our Past: An Introduction to North American Archaeology. *Oxford: Oxford University Press, 2007.*

Northern Arapaho Tribe website: http://www.northernarapaho.com/ Accessed 06.26.2013.

Pettigrew, Dawn K. "Ghost Dances and Identity: Prophetic Religion and American Indian Ethnogenesis in the Nineteenth Century." In Whispering Wind, *July—August, 2012: 30. Accessed via http://go.galegroup.com/ps/i.do?id=GALE%7CA299885330&v=2.1&u=22410_sppl&it=r&p= GPS&sw=w 06.03.2013.*

Shimkin, Demetri. "Eastern Shoshone." In Handbook of North American Indians, *edited by*

William C. Sturtevant, 11:308–335. Washington, DC: Smithsonian Institution, 1986.

Taylor, Colin F. The Plains Indians: A Cultural and Historic View. *New York: Crescent Books, 1994.*

Trenholm, Virginia Cole. The Arapahoes, Our People (Civilization of the American Indian Series). *OK: University of Oklahoma Press, 1986.*

Utley, Robert. Frontiersmen in Blue: The United States Army and the Indians, 1848—1865. *New York: The Macmillan Company, 1967.*

Weist, Katherine M. Plains Indian Woman: An Assessment. *In* Anthropology on the Great Plains. *Lincoln, NB: University of Nebraska Press, 1980.*

Wilson, James. The Earth Shall Weep. *New York: Atlantic Monthly Press, 1998.*

Wind River Indian Reservation website:
http://www.windriver.org/info/communities/reservation.php Accessed 06.26.2013.

12608243R00021

Printed in Great Britain
by Amazon.co.uk, Ltd.,
Marston Gate.